HIGHWAY T L

EDWARD A. FITZPATRICK, *Editor*

Institute of Catechetical Research, Marquette University

THE BOOK OF THE HOLY CHILD

THE BOOK OF THE HOLY CHILD

SISTER MARY BARTHOLOMEW,
O. S. F., B. A., M. A.

ST. AUGUSTINE ACADEMY PRESS
HOMER GLEN, ILLINOIS

Nihil obstat

    H. B. RIES,

        Censor librorum

Imprimatur

    ✠ SAMUEL A. STRITCH,

        Archiepiscopus Milwauchiensis

February 5, 1931

This book was originally published in 1931 by The Bruce Publishing Company.
This edition reprinted in 2017 by St. Augustine Academy Press

Softcover ISBN: 978-1-64051-018-0
Hardcover ISBN: 978-1-64051-019-7

Stories in This Book

Part I

God made the Angels.

God made the moon.
God made the stars.
God made the sea.

God made the land.
God made the sky.
God made the sun.

3

God made the flowers.
God made the trees.
God made the birds.

God made all men.
God made all things.
God made all things for love of us.

God made Adam.
God made Eve.
God made them for heaven.
They were happy.

Adam and Eve did not obey God.
God sent them away. They were
not happy then. God said, "I will
send Jesus from heaven."

God is our Father.
God made me.
God made you.

ROBERT'S PRAYER

Robert said,
"God made all things for us!
How good God is!
Thank You, dear God, thank You!"

HEAVEN

God made me for **heaven.**
I love God.
God made you for **heaven, too.**
Do you love God?
We shall see God in heaven.
We shall be happy in heaven.

Part II

JESUS

This is Jesus.
Jesus loves little boys.
Jesus loves little girls.
Jesus loves me.   I love Jesus.

11

MARY

This is Mary.
Mary is the Mother of Jesus.
Mary is the Blessed Virgin.
Mary is my Mother, too.
I love the Blessed Virgin.

JOSEPH

This is Saint Joseph.
Saint Joseph was a carpenter.
Saint Joseph loved Jesus and Mary.
Saint Joseph loved to work
    for Jesus and Mary.
Saint Joseph loved to pray.

THE HOLY FAMILY

This is the Holy Family,
Jesus, Mary, and Joseph.
Jesus obeyed Mary and Joseph.
He loved to work for Mary
and Joseph.
Joseph was the spouse of Mary

and foster father of Jesus.
Jesus, Mary, and Joseph
   were happy.
Jesus, Mary, and Joseph loved
   to pray.
I love Jesus, Mary, and Joseph.
Jesus, Mary, and Joseph love me.
Jesus, Mary, and Joseph,
   pray for me.
Jesus, Mary, and Joseph,
   I give You my heart
   and my soul.

At Prayer

MY ANGEL

This is an angel.
God gave me an angel.
My angel takes care of me.
I love my angel.
My angel loves me.

Some day I shall see my angel.
I shall see my angel in heaven.

    ❧   ❧   ❧

Oh! my good angel,
Kind and dear!
How glad I am
That you are here.
Stay close by me
All day and night;
And help me do
All that is right.

    ❧   ❧   ❧

Beautiful Angel!
My Guardian so mild,
Tenderly guide me,
For I am thy child.

MY BEST FRIEND

God sent Jesus to live with us.
Jesus is the Son of God.
Jesus loves us.   Jesus wants us
    to be happy in heaven.
Jesus showed us how to get
    to heaven.

The Good Shepherd

20

PART III

THE ANNUNCIATION

Mary lived in Nazareth.
Mary loved to pray.
Mary prayed and prayed
   that the Savior would come.
One day when she was praying,
   an angel came to her.

The angel said:

"Hail, Mary, full of grace!

The Lord is with thee."

The Blessed Virgin was afraid
when she heard the angel.

The angel said to her:

"Fear not, Mary!

You shall have a Son.

His name shall be Jesus."

Mary said: "I will obey.

I am the handmaid of God."

Then Mary went to visit her cousin.

Her cousin said to her:

"Blessed art thou among women."

Mary was happy.

Her cousin was happy, too.

THE ANGELUS

These people were working
  in the field.
The man said,
  "I hear the church bell ringing!"
The woman said, "It is the Angelus.
  Let us pray."
The man and woman were good.

They said the Angelus three times
  each day:
        In the morning,
        At noon, and
        In the evening.
The Angelus is a prayer.
It tells about the Angel's visit
  to Mary.

HAIL, MARY

Hail, Mary, full of grace!
The Lord is with thee.
Blessed art thou among women,
And Blessed is the fruit
  of thy womb, Jesus.
Holy Mary, Mother of God!
Pray for us sinners, now,
And at the hour of our death.
                    Amen.

HOME AT NAZARETH

Mary and Joseph lived at Nazareth.
They worked and prayed.
One day Joseph came home
    from work.
He said to Mary,
"We must go to Bethlehem.

The king has called us."
Mary said, "Let us go.
We must obey the king.
It is God's will."

THE JOURNEY

Mary and Joseph started for
  Bethlehem.
It was far from their home.
Mary and Joseph went along
  the road.

By and by they came to Bethlehem.
It was evening.

Saint Joseph said,
"Let us look for a place to stay."
Saint Joseph went to a house.
A man came to the door.
Saint Joseph said. "May we, please,
come in?"
The man said, "There is no room."
So Mary and Joseph went
from house to house.
No one would take them in.
Saint Joseph was sad.
Mary said, "God will take care
of us."
They went on.
At last they came to a stable.
Mary and Joseph went
into the stable.

They were happy to find a place
  to stay.
"God is good to us," they said,
  "let us thank Him."
"Thank You, dear God!
  Thank You!"

ROSE AND HER MOTHER

Rose liked to play.

One day when she was playing,
Mother said, "Rose, come to me!"

Rose said, "Yes, mother dear,
I will come."

Then she ran to mother.

Rose was a good little girl.

Part IV

The First Christmas

THE FIRST CHRISTMAS

Jesus was born in a stable
  at Bethlehem.
The Blessed Mother put Him
  in the manger.
The Blessed Mother was happy.
Saint Joseph was happy.
God in Heaven was happy.

The angels were happy, too.
Angels came from Heaven
   to the stable.
The angels sang and sang
   to the Infant Jesus.
The angels praised God.
The Blessed Mother and
   Saint Joseph prayed.
They thanked God for giving them
   the Baby Jesus.

LITTLE CHILD IN THE CRIB

I'll always love You, Jesus,
And Mary Mother, too,
And, oh, I hope in heaven
She'll let me play with You.

—*Rev. W. J. Ennis, S. J.*

THE ANNOUNCEMENT

The angels went to call
  the shepherds.
The shepherds were watching
  the sheep.
"Go to Bethlehem," said an angel.

"You will find the Infant Jesus
  in a stable.
He has come down
  from heaven.
He has come
  because He loves you."
Then the angels sang,
  "Glory to God!
    Glory to God!
    Glory to God in the highest!"
The shepherds were very happy.
"Let us go to Bethlehem," they said.
"We want to see the Infant Jesus."
The shepherds went at once
  to Bethlehem.
Their sheep went along
  behind them.
The shepherds found the stable.

They went into the stable.
There they saw the Infant Jesus
   in the manger.
They saw the Blessed Mother
   and Saint Joseph, too.
"How good God is,"
   the shepherds said.
"Let us thank Him."
The shepherds gave thanks to God
   for sending Jesus to them.
They thanked and praised God
   for all the things
   they had seen and heard.
It was just as the Angels
   told them.
They thanked Jesus, too.
They were very, very happy.

The Adoration of the Shepherds

Child:

O sweetest Baby Jesus,
In the manger poor and low,
What can I do to warm You
From the winter's cold and snow!

Infant Jesus:

Dear little child so thoughtful,
I am far from My home above,
So build a crib within your heart,
And warm Me with your love.

—Hope Cecil

ROBERT'S GIFT

Mother told Robert the story
of the shepherds.
Robert said, "I will give Jesus
my rabbit."
"No," said mother,
"Jesus does not want your rabbit.
He wants your love.

If you love Jesus you will often
  visit Him.
When you visit Him in church,
  kneel and say,
'Jesus, I adore You, I love You.'"

GIFTS

All the gifts we see around us
Have been sent us from above.
Let us thank the dear Lord Jesus;
Let us thank Him for His love.

A BOY'S PRAYER

Help me to do the things I should,
To be to others kind and good,
In my work and in my play,
To grow more loving every day.
                    —*Kindergarten Chimes*

THE WONDERFUL STAR

When Jesus was born, three kings
    lived far away.

They were called Wise Men.

One night they saw a bright star
    in the East.

They said, "What a beautiful star!

It tells us that the Savior is born.

Let us go to find Him."
They left their homes.
They followed the star.
They rode for days and days.
At last they came to Jerusalem.
A bad king lived in Jerusalem.
His name was Herod.
The three Kings said to Herod,
"Where is Jesus?
We have seen His star
    and have come to adore Him."

Herod said, "I do not know.

Go, find Jesus,

Then come and tell me.

I want to adore Him, too."

Herod did not want to adore Jesus,
he wanted to kill Him.

The Wise Men followed the star
again.

At last they came to Bethlehem.

"See the star!" said one,

"There it is above the stable!"

The three Wise Men went into the
stable.

There they found Jesus.

They saw the Blessed Mother and
Saint Joseph, too.

They knelt down and adored Jesus.

They said, "God is good!
　Jesus, we adore You
　Jesus, we love You."
Jesus smiled upon them.
They gave Jesus three gifts:
Gold, incense, and myrrh.
They were happy to give Jesus
　something.

❧　　❧　　❧

What can I give to Jesus?
I will give Him my heart.

ROBERT VISITS JESUS

One day, Robert came home from
school and said to his mother,
"The shepherds went to see Jesus.
The Wise Men went to see Jesus.
I want to see Jesus, too.

Where can I find Him?"
His mother said,
"Jesus is in church.
He lives on the altar.
You cannot see Him, now.
You will see Him in heaven.
But, Jesus can see you, now.
He loves to have you visit Him.
It makes Him happy.
You may talk to Him as you talk
    to mother.
He blesses you when you
    visit Him.
And He sends His blessing
    to father and mother."
The next day Robert went
    to church.

Robert said, "Jesus, are You there?
I came to make You happy.
Dear Jesus, I love to visit You.
Bless me and all people.
Good-by, Jesus, I will come again."

MY GIFT

What can I give Him
Poor as I am;
If I were a shepherd,
I would give Him a lamb.
If I were a wise man,
I would do my part.
But what can I give Him?
I will give Him my heart.

— Christina Rossetti

THE RETURN TO THE EAST

An angel came to the Wise Men
at night.
"Do not go back to Herod,"
the angel said.
"He wants to kill Jesus."

The Wise Men obeyed the angel.
They did not go back to King Herod
This made King Herod angry.
He tried to find Jesus.
He sent his men to look for Him.
But they could not find Him.

MY WISH

Do anything You want with me,
Dear God, for I don't care
So long as You will let me love
You always, everywhere!
Do anything You want with me,
Dear God, for it is true
That everything You do is done
To bring me nearer You!

—*Mary Dixon Thayer*

Part V

THE VISIT OF THE ANGEL

One night an angel came to Saint
  Joseph.
The angel said, "Arise, Joseph, take
  the Child and His Mother
  and go into Egypt."

The Flight into Egypt

Saint Joseph obeyed at once.
The Holy Family had to leave
their home.
The Blessed Virgin said,
"God will take care of us.
Let us not be afraid."
Egypt was far away.
It was a long journey.
They went on and on.
They were very tired.
But the Blessed Mother
and Saint Joseph loved Jesus.
They wanted to save Him
from the bad King.
At last they came to Egypt.
They found a home.
The Blessed Virgin and Saint
Joseph thanked God.

IN FAR-AWAY EGYPT

The Holy Family lived in Egypt
a long time.
Saint Joseph worked in his
carpenter shop.
The Blessed Mother worked
in the home.

Jesus grew bigger and stronger.
Joseph loved to work for Jesus
   and Mary.
God took care of the Holy Family.
Jesus, His Blessed Mother,
   and Joseph were happy.

CHRIST OUR KING

The Christ-child stood at Mary's
   knee,
His hair was like a crown,
And all the flowers looked up at
   Him,
And all the stars looked down.
                    — G. K. *Chesterton*

THE RETURN HOME

The Holy Family lived in Egypt
a long, long time.
One night an angel came
to Saint Joseph and said,
"You may go back to your
old home.

He who wanted to kill Jesus
is dead."
Saint Joseph obeyed.
The Blessed Virgin obeyed.
Jesus obeyed, too.
They went back to Nazareth.
They were very happy to be home
again.
"Let us thank God,"
Said the Blessed Mother.
Jesus, His Blessed Mother, and
Saint Joseph knelt down
and thanked God.

HONOR THY FATHER AND THY MOTHER

God wants me to love and obey
my father and mother.

If I love and obey my father and
mother, I shall be happy.

Jesus will love me!

A LITTLE OFFERING

Jesus, to Thee I offer
All I do, and think, and say:
All my work and all my play.
Help me, Jesus, to obey.

Jesus said, "Learn of Me."

Part VI

AT HOME

The little home at Nazareth
    was poor, but the Holy Family
    was happy.
Jesus was kind to His Mother
    and to Saint Joseph.
He helped Saint Joseph
    in the carpenter shop.

He helped the Blessed Mother in
the home.
Jesus, His Blessed Mother, and
Saint Joseph worked very hard.
Jesus did everything His parents
wanted Him to do.
Jesus loved his Blessed Mother
and Saint Joseph.
He obeyed them.

THE CHILD JESUS

Little Jesus, meek and mild,
Pity me, a little child;
Make me humble as Thou art;
For I love Thee with all my heart.

—Author Unknown

THE HAPPY HELPERS

After school Rose and Robert
  help mother.
Rose sweeps the floor and
  sets the table.
Robert goes to the store.
Then they ask,
  "Mother, may we do
    anything else?"

Mother says,
  "You may take care of baby."
After supper Robert brings
  father the paper.
Rose gets father his slippers.
Robert and Rose love and obey
  their father and mother.
They are good children.
They are very happy.
Rose and Robert love Jesus.
They want to be like Jesus
  —happy helpers.

THE LITTLE TEACHER

Some children lived near Jesus.
They often came to see Him.
Jesus was kind to them.
He taught them how to love God.
They listened to Him.
They tried to do all He told them.
This made Jesus happy.

CHILDREN OF THE SHELL

In this picture we see
Jesus and Saint John.
Saint John has been watching
the sheep.
He is tired.
See how kind Jesus is to him.
They loved each other.

A PRAYER

Little Jesus, come to me!
Make a sweet good child of me.
My heart is so small
Thou fillest it all.
There is room for no one
But only Thee.
Dear Little Jesus, stay with me.

At Study

Jesus is God.
He knows all things.
He did not have to study.
He studied to show us
    how to study.
He wants us to study
    to please Him.

Bless my studies!
Bless my work!
All for Thee, dear Jesus!

JESUS AT PRAYER

Jesus loved to pray.
Jesus prayed in the morning!
Jesus prayed during the day.
Jesus prayed at night.
His study, work, and play
    were prayers, because He
    did all for God.

MORNING PRAYER

In the morning when I wake,
I bless myself and say:
"In the name of the Father, and of
    the Son, and of the Holy Ghost,
    Amen.
"Bless me, Dear Jesus, all through
    the day,

Whether I study, work, or play.
To me, Your child, be ever near.
Teach me to love You,
Jesus most dear."

EARLY PRAYER

God, please make me good today
When I work and when I play!

It is easy, God, You see,
For a little child like me

To forget, You always know
What I think, and where I go.

How I act, and that You are sad
Every single time I am bad!

Oh! Please make me good today
When I work, and when I play!

—*Mary Dixon Thayer*

NIGHT PRAYER

"Come, Rose, it is bedtime,"
   said mother.
"Yes, Mother," said Rose,
   "but I must say my prayers."
Rose knelt down near her mother
   and prayed:

Jesus, dearest Jesus, hear me.
Bless Thy little child this night.
In the darkness be Thou near me,
Keep me safe till morning bright.

ॐ　　　ॐ　　　ॐ

AT NIGHT

Help me, dear God, to live the way
You want me to live day by day.
Oh! Show me how to please you
  best
When I'm at work, or play, or rest!
And may I often think of You,
And never say what isn't true,
And never do what isn't right—
I think that's all, dear God,
  Good night!

—*Mary Dixon Thayer*

74

GOOD NIGHT

Good night, dear Lord, and now,
Let them that loved to keep
Thy little bed in Bethlehem
Be near me while I sleep.

—John B. Tabb

ON THE WAY TO JERUSALEM

When Jesus was twelve years old,
He went with His Blessed Mother
   and Saint Joseph to Jerusalem.
The temple was in Jerusalem.
They went there to pray.

They stayed in Jerusalem for four
   or five days.
On the way home Jesus was lost.
The Blessed Mother
   and Saint Joseph were very sad.
They looked for Jesus three days
   and three nights.

At last they went back
    to the temple.
There they found Jesus.
He was teaching the doctors.
The Blessed Mother said to Jesus,
"Son, why hast Thou done so
    to us?"
Jesus said, "Did you not know
I must be about My
    Father's business?"
Jesus went home with His Blessed
    Mother and Saint Joseph.
Jesus obeyed them in all things.

❧   ❧   ❧

You hid Your little Self, dear Lord,
    As other children do;
But, oh, how great was their reward
    Who sought three days for You.

— *Father Tabb*

The Return Home

THE LITTLE SECRET

In this book we have learned
many things about the boy Jesus.
But Jesus, like other boys, soon
grew to be a big boy.
He grew and grew until He was
a man.
We have learned that Jesus,
as a boy, loved and obeyed
His Mother and Saint Joseph.
As Jesus grew older, He was the
same happy Jesus, He always
loved and obeyed His Blessed
Mother and Saint Joseph.
Can you guess why Jesus did all
these things?

Yes, He wished to teach every
    boy and girl His own little secret.
If you love and obey your parents,
    as Jesus did, you know the secret.
Jesus said, "I am the Way,
    the Truth, and the Life;
    Follow Me, your little Leader."

    ❧   ❧   ❧

Jesus, please to help me
In all things I do,
Let me like Your Mother,
Do all things for You.

And Jesus advanced in wisdom,
and age, and grace
with God and men!

"I am the Way, the Truth,
and the Life."

SUGGESTIONS TO THE TEACHER

The Book of the Holy Child is to be used in the First Grade, second semester. The purpose of the book is to instill into the heart of the child a knowledge and a love for the Holy Child, and gratitude for His many gifts. "The most essential thing in life is to love God. The easiest way to love God is to love Him in gratitude. A grateful heart is a loving heart, and a loving heart God never despises."—Father Page.

In order that the material in this book may be of vital value to the child, the teacher must make every effort to arouse and hold the child's interest. And since the keynote of interest is the story, the story method is to be used. First, the story is vividly told by the teacher without the book. Then the picture, or pictures, in the story are studied and discussed, and the child tells the story in his own way. After this, all reading difficulties having been cleared away, the child may read the story and, with the teacher's help, form questions from the story.

Since, as we have mentioned before, the book is intended to create a love for God, and hence, deals with the subject of religion, no reading difficulties should be met with in the Religion class. It will be found that the child is already acquainted with the greater number of words used. The teacher should assist the child in recognizing new words by making deductions from the text, by the use of pictures, phonetics, and all other practical devices. The study of the new words can also be taken up in the word-drill period, using the same method as in reading.

The poems and prayers are to be memorized. However, it is not intended that the child memorize them consciously. By vivid and frequent presentation and discussion, the child will soon know them by heart.

In order that the child may come to think of his religion as a part of his daily life, and not merely as an isolated class, it is well to carry the lessons over into his other schoolwork. Dramatizations and poems may be taken during oral-expression period, some reading during the reading period, illustrations during the art period, and special seat work, based on a particular story in question, assigned during different parts of the day.

The child will enjoy clay modeling and paper cutting to illustrate his own original idea of a story. Interesting seat work can be made in connection with these stories in the form of "yes" and "no" questions, by supplying missing words, by completing sentences, and so forth. These tasks will serve to imprint the stories more firmly upon the mind of the child.

WORD LIST

This word list contains all the different words occurring in the BOOK OF THE HOLY CHILD. The words of the poems and the prayers have been omitted. (See Suggestions to Teachers.) There are 360 words in all. The words in the list are arranged by pages and are marked according to the system used in E. L. Thorndike's *The Teacher's Word Book.* Those from the first 500 words in most common use in reading matter are marked 1a; those from the second 500 are marked 1b; those from the third 500, 2a; those from the fourth 500, 2b, and so forth. Words above the 500 most commonly used are not marked.

1
God	1a
made	1a
the	1a
angel	2a

2
is	1a
our	1a
Father	1a
me	1a
you	1a

3
moon	1b
stars	1b
sea	1a

4
land	1a
sky	1b
sun	1a

5
flower	1a
tree	1a
bird	1a

6
all	1a
men	1a
thing	1a
for	1a
love	1a
of	1a
us	1a

7
Robert	2b
prayer	2a
said	1a
how	1a
good	1a
thank	1a
dear	1a

8
Adam	5a
Eve	3a
them	1a
heaven	1b
they	1a
happy	1a
were	1a

9
and	1a
did	1a
not	1a
obey	2a
sent	1a
away	1a
then	1a
will	1a
send	1a
Jesus	1a
from	1a

10
too	1a
do	1a
we	1a
shall	1a
see	1a
in	1a
be	1a

11
this	1a
little	1a
boy	1a
girl	1a
I	1a

12
Mary	2a
Mother	1a
Bless(ed)	1b
Virgin	3b
my	1a

13
saint	2b
Joseph	3a
was	1a
a	1a
carpenter	3a
to	1a
work	1a
pray	2a

14
Holy	2a
Family	1a
he	1a
spouse	5a

15
foster	5b

16
at	1a

17
an	1a
gave	1a
take	1a
care	1a

18
some	1a
day	1a
side	1a
hear	1a
when	1a
keep	1a
free	1a
every	1a
sin	2b
night	1a

19
best	1a
live	1a
with	1a
Son	1a
wants	1a
show(ed)	1a
get	1a

20
little	1a
child	1a
lead	1a

21
Annunciation	—
Nazareth	—
Savior	5a
would	1a
come	1a
came	1a
her	1a
she	1a

22
Hail	2b
full	1a
grace	1b
Lord	1b
Thee	1b
art	1b
thou	1b
among	1a
women	2a
afraid	1b
heard	1a
fear	1a

have	1a		house	1a		just	1a		but	1a
his	1a		door	1a		told	1b		now	1a
name	1a		may	1a		*37*			make	1a
am	1a		please	1a		adoration	—		talk	1a
handmaid	—		there	1a		*39*			as	1a
went	1a		no	1a		gift	1b		next	1a
visit	1a		room	1a		story	1a		*47*	
cousin	2a		sad	1b		rabbit	2b		are	1a
23			on	1a		does	1a		people	1a
Angelus	—		last	—		your	1a		Good-by	3b
these	1a		stable	2b		*40*			*49*	
field	1a		*29*			if	1a		return	1b
man	1a		find	1a		often	1a		back	1a
church	1a		*30*			kneel	3b		*50*	
bell	1b		Rose	1b		say	1a		angry	2a
ring(ing)	1b		like(d)	1a		adore	4a		tried	2a
woman	1a		play	1a		*41*			could	1a
it	1a		yes	1b		wonderful	1b		*51*	
let	1a		ran	1b		wise	1b		arise	3a
24			*31*			bright	1b		Egypt	3a
three	1a		first	1a		east	1a		*52*	
times	1a		Christmas	1b		what	1a		flight	2b
each	1a		*32*			beautiful	1a		*53*	
morning	1a		born	1b		*42*			leave	1a
noon	1b		put	1a		left	1a		long	1a
evening	1b		him	1a		followed	1a		tired	1b
tell(s)	1a		manger	5b		rode	2b		save	1a
about	1a		*33*			Jerusalem	—		*54*	
25			sang	2b		bad	1a		shop	1b
home	1a		baby	1b		Herod	—		*55*	
one	1a		praise(d)	2a		where	1a		grew	1b
must	1a		give(ing)	1a		*43*			bigger	1a
go	1a		*34*			know	1a		stronger	
Bethlehem	—		Announcement	–		kill	1a		(strong)	1a
26			shepherd(s)	2b		again	1a		took	1a
king	1a		watch(ing)	1a		above	1a		*56*	
has	1a		sheep	1b		knelt	1b		old	1a
call(ed)	1a		*35*			*44*			*57*	
journey	1b		down	1a		smile(d)	1a		who	1a
start(ed)	1a		because	1a		upon	1a		dead	1a
far	1a		glory	2a		gold	2a		*58*	
their	1a		high(est)	1a		incense	1a		honor	1b
along	1a		very	1a		myrrh	—		thy	2a
road	1a		once	1a		something	1a		children	1a
27			behind	1a		can	1a		always	1a
by	1a		found	1a		heart	1a		*60*	
28			*36*			*45*			learn	1a
look	1a		into	1a		school	1a		*61*	
place	1a		saw	1a		*46*			poor	1a
stay	1a		seen	1a		altar	3b		kind	1a

62		paper	1a	*72*		so	1a
hard	1a	slippers		whether	1b	business	1b
everything	1b	(slipper)	3b	ever	1a	*80*	
parents		*65*		most	1a	secret	2a
(parent)	2a	teacher	1b	*73*		book	1a
soul	1b	near	1a	bedtime	—	many	1a
63		often	1a	*76*		soon	1a
after	1a	taught	2a			until	1a
help	1a	listened	2a	way	1a	same	1a
sweeps		*66*		twelve	1b	guess	1b
(sweep)	2b	shell	2a	years (year)	1a	*81*	
floor	1a	picture	1a	temple	2b	wished	
sets (set)	1a	John	1a	*77*		(wish)	1a
table	1a	been	1a	stay(ed)	1a	every	1a
goes	2b	other	1a	four	1a	own	1a
store	1b	*68*		five	1a	truth	1b
ask	1a	study	1b	lost	1a	life	1a
may	1a	*70*		*78*		leader	2a
anything	1b	during	1a	teaching	1b	*83*	
else	1b	*71*		doctors		advanced	
64		wake	2a	(doctor)	1b	(advance)	2a
says (say)	1a	myself	1b	hast	3b	wisdom	2a
supper	2a	Ghost	2b	done	1a	age	1b
brings	1a	Amen	—			grace	1b
		through	1a				